Introducing Anglican Beliefs

by

ROY HERBERT

Training Tutor, Church of England Youth Council

1962

CHURCH INFORMATION OFFICE

CHURCH HOUSE, WESTMINSTER, SWI

ΧΡΙΣΤΟΦΕΡΩ

ΑΓΑΠΗ ΚΑΙ ΕΥΧΑΡΙΣΤΙΑ

COMMENDATION

I gladly commend this statement of essential Anglican beliefs. I hope that it may do much good by helping young people and stimulating them to further study.

Michael Cantuar:

FOREWORD

This book has been written for young people thinking seriously about the Christian faith as held by the Church of England, but I believe it deserves to reach and will be welcomed by a much wider public, amongst which there might well be members of churches, traditions and persuasions other than our own. In this way it will serve the cause of Christian unity.

It is written with the reverence of a true son of the Church, who writes with the knowledge and authority given to those who sincerely practise their faith. With this, and a rare sympathy and understanding of other traditions, Mr Herbert has written a book which will help all who read it—young and old—to a deeper and more intelligent understanding of the Christian faith.

+Edward Bath et Well:

Chairman of the Church of England Youth Council

PREFACE

THIS book is an expansion of some notes originally prepared, at the request of the Church of England Youth Council, for the Anglican delegates to the Ecumenical Youth Assembly in Europe 1960 at Lausanne and more recently used as preparatory material for the Third British Conference of Christian Youth at Leicester.

Earlier this year the Publications Committee of the Church of England Board of Education suggested that the material should be printed and made available to a wider public. In preparing it for publication it became clear that note-form should give way to more continuous prose and that the bare bones of doctrinal statement needed some appropriate clothing.

The result is far from adequate and is intended to be only an *introduction* to the Anglican position. It presupposes a willingness on the part of the reader to explore other more detailed works in order to extend his grasp of the subject. I hope he will be encouraged in this by the classified reading list at the end of the book.

He will not necessarily find the following pages easy reading. That is not the objective. He will need to read carefully and thoughtfully. In doing so I hope he may begin to glimpse something of the true nature of the Church of England. That would be reward enough for daring to write about her essential beliefs.

To write of them in so short a compass is not an enviable task. But it has been a labour of love. I love the Church of England. I am proud of her incomparable heritage and thankful for what I believe to be her present glory and her future hope. If those who read this book have their love deepened through the understanding, it may not perhaps have been written in vain.

Love for a particular Church, however, is partial. It cannot be otherwise while Christians are divided. So we must draw nearer to each other. In his infinite wisdom our Heavenly Father already knows the solution to the problems of our disunity. In so far as we draw nearer to him, through our Lord Jesus Christ and in the power of the Holy Spirit, we grow in holiness and truth. By these gifts our partial love may be made whole. By them we may all come to the unity for which Christ prayed.

Finally I must thank all those who have helped me in so many ways:—

First, my humble thanks to the Archbishop of Canterbury for his kindness in finding time in a crowded programme to read both the original notes and the typescript of the book. I am very grateful for the generosity and care with which he has guided and helped me, and for his commendation of the book to young people for whom it was specially but not exclusively written.

Next I am grateful to my Chairman, the Bishop of Bath and Wells, for the encouragement he has given me from the beginning and for his more than generous Foreword.

My thanks are due also to the Bishop of Rochester, the Reverend Kenneth Slack, General Secretary of the British Council of Churches, and to the Reverend David Jenkins, Chaplain of The Queen's College, Oxford. All of them were kind enough to read the first draft and to offer comments and criticisms.

I am particularly indebted to Canon Noel Kennaby, Senior Chaplain to the Archbishop of Canterbury, who has read the book at all stages and made many helpful suggestions. His wise counsel, given under pressure of the printing timetable, has been encouragement indeed.

Last but not least, a word of sincere appreciation for the patience and wisdom with which my colleague, Miss Rachel Hadow, Secretary of the Church of England Youth Council, has lived with the draft over recent weeks, and for the perseverence of my secretary, Mrs. Janet Neale, in typing more drafts than I care to remember.

Trinity, 1962   ROY HERBERT

CONTENTS

The Cover

The cover picture is of the Gethsemane Chapel in the new Coventry Cathedral. The beautiful mosaic represents the Angel of the Agony holding the cup of suffering and the bronze screen represents the crown of thorns. The colour photograph is reproduced by courtesy of Shell-Mex and B.P. Ltd.

1

THE CHURCH

The People of God
The Body of Christ
One, Holy, Catholic and Apostolic

The People of God

MANY who are ready enough to hear about Jesus stop listening when the Church is mentioned. Why drag in the Church? Simply because you cannot talk about Jesus without talking about the Church too.

Of course the image of the Church is often distorted. It is sometimes that of an ancient building which is costly to maintain; sometimes that of an institution which breaks down; sometimes that of a limited but by no means perfect hierarchy of parsons.

The men and women who fill the pages of the New Testament would be tolerantly amused at these ideas. They would perhaps agree that we should begin with the Church, but they would add unhesitatingly that this means beginning with *people*.

It is *people* who make life exciting. The Church is exciting, too, because it is concerned with and indeed is made up of *people* of all kinds – old and young, good and bad, living and departed. In theological terms this means the *People of God* or, to quote the revised Catechism, the *Family of God*. This does not at all imply that they are spiritually or morally superior to others; rather that they are called by God to undertake the most exciting task in the world – a task best understood in the light of St. Paul's description of the Church as the *Body of Christ*.

The Body of Christ

This is a vivid metaphor given to us by a lively writer who, unlike doubting Thomas, had no opportunity to see or touch the human form of Jesus. Yet Paul clearly realised that it was through his human Body that God himself spoke to men and was *active in the world in recognizable form* – among men as man. He went on to grasp the truth that after the Ascension Christ's work did not come to an end. On the contrary, it was continued through a small group of young men commissioned by Christ for this task. They have been succeeded over the centuries by millions who have entered the Church through Baptism so that we to-day are indeed the *Body of Christ* called by him to be *active in the world in recognizable form* on his behalf. We are thus his eyes to see men's needs; his lips to speak God's message of love; his hands to minister to men; his feet to walk in his footsteps; his heart filled with compassion; his mind to grow in wisdom.

In his power and after his likeness the Church is *people* caring for *people*, seeking to love and to serve and to reconcile. The light of this love and service and reconciliation is so to shine in the world that men may come to glorify God. Men are to see God in us and come to God through us. This is the purpose and function of the Church. This is our task. Unless we start here we cannot begin to speak of that branch of the Church which historically has its roots in English soil.

Her nature as well as her purpose and function are described in the Creeds. Through the public confession of the Apostles' Creed in Morning and Evening Prayer and of the Nicene Creed in the Service of Holy Communion the Church of England claims to witness to and be part of the *One*, *Holy*, *Catholic and Apostolic* Church. These phrases are known collectively as the *marks* of the Church and we must consider them in detail.

'One . . . .'

The Church is one, first in relation to God himself:

> ONE with God through Christ in Scripture, Creeds, Sacraments and Ministry, derived from the primitive undivided Church.

Belief in the oneness of the Church despite her divisions is fundamental because it was God who called her into being – *Ye have not chosen me*, said Jesus, *but I have chosen you*. Herein lies not only her derived authority but also her abiding unity. It is thus of her nature that she is one family under one Father.

Next she is one internally, so to speak:

> ONE, that is, UNITED in herself, not in a dull uniformity, but in a rich diversity.

The Church has never been an unimaginative monochrome. The twelve Apostles were men of widely differing temperaments and opinions. Real unity is not a levelling-out process, but a growing in love which binds together many different strands in one unbreakable whole. Party labels and differences of churchmanship are insignificant compared with common loyalty to our Heavenly Father. This unity in diversity is not maintained without the healthy tension which strengthens discipline and deepens love. So it must surely be in a re-united Church.

Finally the Church also expresses her belief in ultimate and complete unity of all Christian people:

> ONE also in the sense in which our Lord prayed 'that they all may be one', expressing the fundamental belief that the true Church is characterized by a unity of all Christian people everywhere, whose present divisions are a scandal to be removed by love and wisdom born of prayer.

A pious hope! So the sceptic may comment. The hope, however, is quickened as the Church sets about her duty to follow her Master in praying and working constantly for this end. Under the Holy Spirit her efforts have borne much fruit in recent years. Many things still remain undone. So long as they do she must continue to proclaim her belief and to match it with appropriate action.

'. . . . Holy'

It is not arrogance but the truth which impels the Church to lay claim to holiness. She makes the claim in two senses. First:

> *HOLY in the sense that it is of divine origin and not simply man-made; whose Head is Christ himself.*

The first Apostles did not choose themselves; our Lord chose them as a team and trained them first to share and then to inherit his earthly ministry. They became what they were as a result of his initiative. The Church is the Church to-day for the same reason. It was the divine command to *follow me* which started it all. It was the divine commission *go ye forth* . . . . which is the Church's authority. The Church is God-given and so holy. Only this could justify St Paul's descriptive phrase *The Body of Christ*.

To complete the metaphor, the Head of the Body is Christ himself. The intimate and personal relationship which should exist between Head and Body is implicit in the second sense in which the Church claims holiness:

> *HOLY also in the sense of separated for God's use, and so consecrated to God's service in this world and beyond.*

To be holy is to be whole. The Church's wholeness lies in

her humble yet privileged role as the instrument of God's purpose in the world. She cannot fulfil this role unless she is for ever in intimate touch with Christ her Head. Once let the body lose touch with the head and it is out of control and ineffective. This attachment to God in Christ is the basis of the Church's claim to be holy. She thus stands foursquare with God in order that she may be very much in the world as his instrument. She is thus called to experience the complex interplay between the interior life of the soul, where holiness is nurtured, and the exterior throbbing life of the world, where holiness is the leaven in the lump.

'. . . . Catholic'

The word is much misunderstood but for all that it is firmly entrenched in the Creeds of our Church. Our Prayer Book also contains the prayer for 'the good estate of the Catholic Church' as well as the Bidding 'Pray for Christ's Holy Catholic Church'. Its original sense may be defined as follows:

> *CATHOLIC, that is UNIVERSAL, for all men in all places and at all times.*

God's love extends to all his creatures without exception. The Church as God's continuing redemptive agency in the world is no less universal. No one section of the Church of God can lay sole claim to this description. All must strive towards a universal cherishing of the Faith in its fulness. Failure to do this, not time and space, is what divides. Men at different times and in widely separated places will accept the Catholic claim of the Church in so far as the Faith in its fulness is presented.

The treasuring and careful preservation of the whole Faith has produced a second meaning of the word Catholic:

> *CATHOLIC, that is, HOLDING THE HISTORIC FAITH derived in unbroken line from the Church of the Apostles.*

In this sense it signifies orthodoxy as opposed to unorthodox deviations from the true Faith. In the 16th century the zeal of the Church in this land for reform was matched by great care in the retention of the essential elements of the Faith of the Catholic and undivided Church. As a result she has retained her belief in the authority and inspiration of Scripture, her profession of the Catholic Creeds, her faithful administration of the Dominical Sacraments and her Ministry intact and in unbroken line.

'. . . . and Apostolic'

The Church claims to be Apostolic in the sense that:

> *She is SENT into all the world proclaiming the Apostolic Faith handed down under the Holy Spirit and within the CONTINUITY of the Church in history. This continuity is seen in the unbroken succession of her threefold Ministry of Bishops, Priests and Deacons which is the principle of unity in teaching and sacraments.*

The key words are *sent* and *continuity*. The root meaning of the word 'apostle' is *sent*. An apostle was a messenger. So is the Church. She is *sent* to preach the Gospel to all the world. She is thus in her nature and function a missionary body. She is untrue to her calling if for a moment she ceases to be this. Archbishop Temple put it succinctly when he spoke of the Church as *existing for the sake of those who are not yet her members*.

She cannot do this unless what she proclaims is true and the sacraments she offers are real sacraments. So it has always been a charge upon the Church to safeguard the *continuity* of teaching and sacraments. The early Church as described in the Acts of the Apostles certainly *continued steadfastly in the Apostle's teaching . . . . and in breaking of bread*. Since then the Church has tried to do the same through a *continuing* Ministry of Bishops, as the Apostles' successors and heirs, Priests and Deacons. The precious heritage of teaching and sacrament is regarded as *handed down* from the Apostles to succeeding generations of bishops in unbroken line. At the Reformation particular care was taken to ensure that Archbishop Parker should be consecrated by bishops all of whom had been duly consecrated in this line.

Both in a reaching-out, which expresses the 'sentness' of her mission, and in a stretching-back, which marks a proper care for her inheritance of doctrine and sacrament, the Church is Apostolic.

2

AN ANGLICAN APPROACH
TO UNITY

The Search for Truth
The Lambeth Quadrilateral

The Search for Truth

IN the Bidding Prayer mentioned in the first chapter Christ's Holy Catholic Church is described as *the whole congregation of Christian people dispersed throughout the whole world*. The people are dispersed. The Church is divided. The Body is broken. The unity Christ prayed for has been shattered by a world-wide fragmentation. Catholic universal oneness can be claimed in its entirety by no single section of the whole congregation.

The fragmentation is not simply one of organization; it is primarily a fragmentation of the truth. Disunity is the result of a departure from holiness through sin, which obscures the truth. The mind of Christ, which St Paul suggests should be informing Christian thinking, has been progressively blurred. As sinful men, no matter how apparently sincere their motives, have exalted their own conception of the truth to the point of principle and irrevocable decision, so limb after limb of the Body-whole has been torn off, more often in anger than in sorrow.

The world, for whom Christ prayed that unity might be a way to believe, thus sees a dismembered Body; many different Churches preaching many different things. Instead of belief there is confusion which so often leads to apathy and disbelief. Disbelief is the world's judgment on the Church. And who is to blame the world, for it surely senses the lie that is presented – the partial truth, the broken Body, the dismembered Christ?

In our separate denominations we have been living this lie for many generations. Only in recent years has it become an uncomfortable role. The more uncomfortable it becomes the greater the hope of recovering the whole truth and of its acceptance by the world. The lie must be nailed by a fearless search for the truth as it is in Jesus. It is this search which is at the heart of an approach to unity.

We cannot all be right: we may all in varying degrees be wrong. Only the truth will set us free to see clearly where we stand with God and with each other. To reach out towards the truth in its wholeness will be hard. We are not only faced with a confusing array of extant versions of the Christian Faith, but are also called to an ultimate unity in Christ which comprehends all without exception in one visible Body.

The Lambeth Quadrilateral

Few would quarrel with this as the ultimate goal. It presupposes an honest assessment of just where each Church stands. We must speak the truth in love to each other and truth, like charity, may best begin at home. So we need first to be clear as to how we see the truth as it appears to have been retained in our own Church.

As long ago as the Lambeth Conference of 1884 the Anglican Church stated what it considered to be of the truth in her own Communion and what, therefore, she regarded as desirable in a re-united Church. The statement is known as the Lambeth Quadrilateral and was included in a revised form in the *Appeal to all Christian People* in 1920.

It is no accident that the four points of the statement are concerned with what we believe to be the Catholic inheritance of the Church and that they are enshrined in the two great gifts of the Reformation, namely the English Bible and the English Prayer Book. The statement thus bears witness to the nature of the Church of England as both Catholic and Reformed. It is concerned with:

  (i) *The Holy Scriptures*

  (ii) *The Nicene and Apostles' Creeds*

  (iii) *The Sacraments of Baptism and Holy Communion*

  (iv) *The historic threefold Ministry of Bishops, Priests and Deacons*

True and visible unity presupposes more than a loose confederation of churches. The search for it usually assumes a large measure of agreement of essential doctrine and the acceptance of a common authority before, rather than after, participation in sacramental fellowship at the altar, save in exceptional circumstances. This has tended to be prominent in Anglican thinking about the path to unity. It is not surprising, therefore, that the Lambeth Quadrilateral tells us explicitly of four areas in which agreement is regarded as essential. Outside them there is by implication room for a wide variety of practice and custom. We have first, however, to strive under the Holy Spirit to discover and agree together on the truth in these areas of common concern.

There is the rub. It is the discovery of the truth, even in these specific areas, which constitutes the major task of all who long for unity. Definition is the root difficulty. Some hold that the Church, as Christ intends it, is not to be found where there is error in any of the four areas or where there is omission of one of them. Others maintain that God overrules our sins and that the Church is to be found elsewhere, even though this is to greater or less degree defective. All, however, would agree that, looking to the future and the building up of the divided Church, all these areas must find space in the pattern of total unity.

We need then to look more closely at each of them in turn. The Anglican, examining his faith and practice in company with others of different persuasions, will be wise to come back again and again to these four areas in which common agreement as to the truth is essential.

The discussion which follows cannot, in so short a space, do full justice either to the Anglican position or to that of other churches. It is intended, as the Archbishop states in his commendation, simply as an aid and stimulus to further study.

3

THE THREEFOLD APPEAL

Scripture
Tradition
Reason
Other Churches

IN considering the first part of the Lambeth Quadrilateral referring to Scripture we must look in turn at Tradition and Reason as well. It is this threefold appeal to *Scripture*, *Tradition* and *Reason* which is the distinctive Anglican approach to matters of essential doctrine.

The Holy Scriptures

The Revised Catechism describes the Bible as being, both in the Old and New Testaments:

> The record of God's revelation of himself to mankind through his people Israel, and above all in his Only Son, Jesus Christ.

As such it has a prominent place in the worship of our Church. Our manual of worship, the Book of Common Prayer, is the result of a skilful welding of old liturgical forms with the new English Bible under the genius of Thomas Cranmer. Hardly any public service takes place without the reading of portions of the Bible; the prayers, exhortations and responses of the Prayer Book are filled with biblical phrases, often of great beauty. No wonder it has been said that the Church of England may claim to be in her worship the most biblical Church in Christendom.

This is no accident for it was made abundantly clear at the Reformation that the Bible is the ultimate sanction for all our teaching. It is in fact what Bishop Headlam used to call the Title Deeds of our Faith. All doctrinal statements including the Creeds are to be brought to this test. The Sixth Article in the Book of Common Prayer asserts:

> Holy Scripture containeth all things necessary to salvation: so that whatsoever is not read therein nor may be proved thereby is not to be required of any man that it should be believed as an Article of the Faith or be thought requisite or necessary to salvation.

The priest at his ordination gives an undertaking to teach nothing as necessary to salvation which is not contained in Scripture. The bishop at his consecration gives a similar undertaking in even more emphatic terms.

Other opinions and customs may sincerely be held and practised, but unless they meet this test they must not be regarded, still less taught, as essential.

The Tradition of the Church

Christian men and women, however, came before Christian books. Long before the earliest New Testament letters were written the Church was proclaiming the Gospel. It was in and through the life and work of the Church that the books were written. Later they came to be understood and received as her official documents.

As they were inspired by the Holy Spirit within the life of the Church, so under the same Spirit they have been handed down and interpreted by the Church. This handing down, providing as it does for continuity and consistency in teaching, we call Tradition. It ensures the preservation of the same essential truths and their handing over to successive generations.

The appeal to Tradition has long been a principle of our Church which holds in special respect the writings of the Early Fathers. These were the theologians who wrote during the formative period of Christian doctrine in the first five centuries. This emphasis is illustrated by a Canon of 1571 which indicates that the teaching of the clergy should be consistent with that of *the Catholic Fathers and the ancient bishops*. In England the Reformers' desire to move in accordance with the Tradition of the Early Fathers undoubtedly steadied the movement and saved it from some of the extravagancies of continental reform. Cranmer himself appealed to it in defence of changes in doctrinal statements and forms of worship.

Tradition is not of course a rival or an alternative authority to the Scriptures. It serves simply to make clearer what the Scriptures say to us through the corporate mind of the Church. Reverence for Tradition expresses the belief that the Holy Spirit has continued to enable the Church to make sense of 'the things concerning Jesus' which are the heart of the Gospel. It is in this sense that we accept the ancient principle that the Church is the guardian and interpreter of the Scriptures under the guidance of the Holy Spirit.

Reason

The third appeal is to Reason. It may be that in any given instance a clear Tradition is lacking. There may be disagreement between two or more Fathers. There may even have been a mistaken exegesis revealed by later research. Reason given to us by God must then be used to weigh the evidence and come to a conclusion.

Accordingly our Faith, shaped as we believe by Scripture

and Tradition, may legitimately be tested by the reasoning processes of the mind. The appeal to sound learning has always been a feature of the Anglican Church and it has produced a long line of scholars and divines. Butler and Berkeley in the 18th century, Lightfoot and Westcott in the 19th century and many more in the 20th century have all used the weapons of Reason to grapple with new discoveries and fresh modes of thought. Through their appeal to sound learning it has been made clear that Reason does not run contrary to revelation in the search for truth.

For the Anglican, Catholicism is not static but progressive. It has no fear of new discoveries. All truth, however new to man, is but a further revelation of the truth that is in God.

The same principle holds for the man in the pew as for the theological scholar. The ordinary member in the Church of England has little in the way of authoritative statements from above to guide him. The authority of the Church is like that of our Lord's. It permits of questioning and doubts; it respects personality and rejoices only when obedience is consistent with conscience and conviction and, therefore, with Reason. As in the Church of the Early Fathers it is restricted to Scriptural principles. Their application breeds an intellectual climate which is stimulating, and there is plenty of room for movement. For most of her members this is one of her glories and, in the context of ecumenical discussion, one of her challenges.

Conclusion

We have seen that the authority of our Faith is found in the threefold appeal:

(i) *to Holy Scripture, written by men inspired by the Holy Spirit;*
(ii) *to the Tradition of the Church under the Holy Spirit;*
(iii) *to Reason which is itself the gift of the Holy Spirit.*

The references to the Holy Spirit are important. They indicate the interaction between the Spirit on the one hand and man, whether as an individual or as a Church, on the other. As Archbishop Fisher has put it:

'The Church of England believes that the Holy Spirit of God, the only final authority, speaks to us—

in Holy Scripture
in the Tradition of the Church, and
in the living thought and experience of to-day . . . .

. . . . and we believe that, in the fellowship of charity and worship, the Holy Spirit will keep us in the true Faith.'

Other Churches

Different Churches place different emphases on the respective roles of Scripture, Tradition and Reason in determining the Faith. Some tend to place Scripture on a lonely summit out of reach of the other two. Some give greater freedom to the exercise of Reason, while others tend to restrict it.

The Roman Church holds Tradition in high esteem and has the additional institutional arrangement whereby the Papacy is the instrument for defining and declaring the Faith.

These differences raise the fundamental question of the nature of *authority*, that is, precisely what is the *authority* by which a Church formulates its expression of the Christian Faith and determines the manner and scope of her life in the world ?

4

THE CREEDS

THE three remaining articles of the Lambeth Quadrilateral refer to the Creeds, the Sacraments and the Ministry of the Church. Each of them has its place in the worship of the Church. All three will be more fully understood if we recognize them as essential pieces of the pattern and texture of the Prayer Book.

A Handbook of Doctrine

The Book of Common Prayer is more than a manual of worship. It is also a handbook of Anglican doctrine. Though this is sometimes forgotten, it is not surprising. We have already seen how its language and style are biblical through and through. We have seen too that it bears explicit witness to the priority of Scripture in the formulation of true doctrine. Worship is thus the living context in which doctrine is expressed. So the regular churchman may over the years experience the reiteration of accepted doctrines and come to have their meaning for him deepened and his convictions about them strengthened.

In Morning and Evening Prayer and in the Service of Holy Communion he is reminded of the central Christian beliefs through the corporate recitation of the Creeds. In Baptism Christ's redeeming action through his Church is proclaimed. By learning the Catechism in preparation for Confirmation he is taught the sacramental nature of the Church's function. As a communicant member he grows in the experience of the truth of this. In the *Ordering of*

Bishops, Priests and Deacons he hears set forth the doctrine of a continuing Ministry stretching back through the Apostles to Christ himself.

Worship is the Church's highest duty. In this setting the dry bones of formal doctrinal statement come alive. The worshipper may thus gradually recognize the Prayer Book as an extension and clarification of biblical truth. He may come to realize the nature of the Church as the Family of God, for it is as a member of a congregation that he has his own part to play in the expression of belief. He may also begin to grasp something of the comprehensiveness of the Church as ancient Catholic phrases are used side by side with the more recent additions of the Reformers.

It is all there for him who has ears to hear and eyes to see. The Anglican who wishes to be knowledgeable about the Faith will use the Book of Common Prayer as a basic text book alongside the Bible. With this in mind we turn first to the Creeds.

The Apostles' Creed

The Reformers claimed that they were attempting to re-establish the practices and standards of the primitive Church. They had no intention therefore of formulating new Creeds. It was more appropriate to retain the Creeds of the Early Church, the most ancient of which is the Apostles' Creed.

This was the old Roman Creed dating from the 2nd century. It is still the Baptismal Creed of the Church today and is used to determine the candidate's loyalty to the established Faith of the Church to which he seeks admission.

It is the simplest of our Creeds. Probably because of its

recitation in Morning and Evening Prayer, it is also the most familiar.

It is a largely factual statement of our belief in the Trinity and the Church. It may be paraphrased as follows:

We believe in a personal God who is Father of all and Creator of all men and all things;

We believe in Jesus Christ who is both God and man, and who came to live for a time among men in order to do three things:

to show the true character of God in relation to man; and the true character of man in relation to God;

to bring into the world the Power of God that, through his Love and Sacrifice, he might overcome evil and deliver all men from it; and

to make that Power active in all who believe in him.

All this he did, once and for all, in his Life and Death and in his glorious Resurrection and Ascension;

We believe in the Holy Spirit who works specially, but not exclusively, within the society of those who believe in Jesus; in this society men are called to experience the presence and guidance of the Spirit, and through this society the redeeming work of Christ is continued, not in the sense of being added to but in the sense of being made continuously available and active in succeeding generations of men;

Further, this society we call the Holy Catholic Church of which Christ himself is the Head, and which is partly militant here on earth and partly triumphant in the eternal Kingdom of God, to which Christ brings all faithful men, there to glorify and enjoy him for ever.

The Nicene Creed

This Creed was formulated in the 4th century. It is Eastern in origin. As such it is not so much concerned with facts as with the interpretation of facts and their formulation in theological language. This was made necessary at a time when strange and unorthodox ideas about the Person of our Lord were being canvassed.

It is very much a defence of the Faith with particular reference to the divinity of Jesus Christ. Hence the longer central paragraph elaborating the description of our Lord as *God of God, Light of Light . . . . being of one substance with the Father*.

It quickly became the Creed used at the Eucharist both in the East and the West. The corporate profession of it in our Service of Holy Communion has made it familiar to Englishmen. We hold this detailed expression of central belief in common with other Christians of the Roman and Eastern Orthodox Churches.

The Athanasian Creed

Unlike the other two Creeds, this one is not the fruit of the collective mind of the Church. It is the work of one person, though not St Athanasius to whom it has for so long been ascribed.

Our Church continues to honour it as a valuable theological statement. But its language is too technical for popular use and its damnatory phrases are open to misunderstanding.

Accordingly, along with the Eastern and Roman Churches, its use in public worship is not insisted upon, nor is it included in the second of the articles of the Lambeth Quadrilateral. The Apostles' Creed and its extension in the more detailed phrases of the Nicene Creed adequately state the Anglican position.

Other Churches

There is a wide measure of agreement between all the main Christian bodies that the Apostles' Creed sets forth the substance of the Christian Faith. Recognition of this fact in recent times is a thing to be thankful for.

The Orthodox, Roman and Lutheran Churches all recognize both the Apostles' and Nicene Creeds, though the former has never been officially used in the East.

The Presbyterian Church and the English Free Churches are traditionally less happy about their regular use in liturgical worship. They are hesitant about regarding them as a standard by which personal belief may be tested, though there is wide agreement about them as a formal standard for the belief of the Church as a whole.

5

INTRODUCTION TO THE SACRAMENTS

Unity of Word and Sacrament

THE Church's Ministry is one of both Word and Sacrament. As the Word is proclaimed in the public reading and exposition of the Bible, so the Sacraments are celebrated and made regularly available to men.

Particular parties may emphasize sometimes the Word and sometimes the Sacraments. Yet the Church of England ever stands for the faithful dispensation of both parts of her Ministry. Symbols of this exist in every church. Pulpit and lectern remind us of Scripture: font and altar of the Sacraments.

Her double function is clearly demonstrated in the service of Holy Communion. An essential part of the rite is the reading of Scripture in Epistle and Gospel and its exposition in the address.

The whole service is thoroughly biblical in style and content. Word and Sacrament are shown to be intimately related. The eucharistic action of the whole Church, gathered for worship, is one of the important ways in which the essential unity of her twofold Ministry is proclaimed.

Greater and Lesser Sacraments

This unity is underlined by the Church's witness to the two essential Sacraments. They are *Baptism* and *Holy Communion*. Both derive from Scripture. Both were directly instituted and ordained by Christ himself. St Matthew tells us of our Lord's command to baptize all nations: both the Gospel writers and St Paul record his command to perpetuate the Last Supper. These are sometimes called *the greater Sacraments*.

Five other Sacraments are sometimes called *the lesser Sacraments*. They are *Confirmation* which has close connections with Baptism as we shall see later; *Ordination* or the Ordering of Bishops, Priests and Deacons; *Holy Matrimony* in which God joins together husband and wife *so long as they both shall live*; the *Ministry of Absolution* in which after confession and true repentance man may receive the assurance of God's forgiveness with spiritual counsel and advice; and the *Ministry of Healing* in which the Church continues Christ's work among the sick through the laying on of hands with prayer. These do not come in the same category as the *greater Sacraments*, since they are not directly attributable to Christ's command.

Means of Grace

All Sacraments, however, are used and experienced within the life and worship of the Church. Through them the life of the Church is sustained by God; through them Christ risen and alive is active in his Body; through them the Holy Spirit sheds abroad in our hearts the love of God. In short they are means of grace: God's method of endowing us with the gifts we need to live as he knows best and to fulfil the work he has given us to do.

In Baptism we enter the invigorating stream of the new

and risen life of Christ our Head. As an essential part of this new life we are constantly fed and nourished by his Body and Blood in Holy Communion. So the Sacraments bear eloquent witness to our Lord's own words: *Apart from me ye can do nothing.* He is the Vine; we are the branches. In so far as we abide in him, in and through the Sacraments, the Church becomes in truth the continuing, crucified, risen and glorified Body of Christ in his world.

Visible Marks of the Visible Church

God, in his infinite compassion, is understanding of man's need for tangible, visible signs of the truth. The great proof of this is our Lord's condescension in coming to live among men as man. Only so could the majesty of God become meaningful to man in his fallen lack of majesty. Only so could God speak to man in terms he could understand, whether he heard or whether he chose to be deaf. Only so could the Love of God be recognized as the initiative which gives until it can give no more, whether it be accepted or not. Only so could man see himself as he can become in fellowship with God, whether he desires it or whether he rejects it. Here was God, visible, tangible, Creator, Father, Saviour, Sanctifier; and here was man, the creature truly reflecting the image of God, veritable son, saved and sanctified.

These still astonishing facts of Christ's earthly life lie behind William Temple's assertion that Christianity is the most materialistic of all religions. As it was in our Lord's Ministry on earth, so it is in the sacramental life of the Church to-day. As the human body of Christ conveyed the truth of God's character and man's destiny, so the Sacraments through water in Baptism and through bread and wine in Communion convey the same truths. They are *outward and visible signs of an inward and spiritual grace*. By them God's love is offered to man. Man in his response and acceptance may come more nearly to reflect the image of God which is his inheritance.

So the signs are not only outward and visible. They are also *effectual* signs conveying to man God's grace: his gifts of love, joy, peace, strength, wholeness and fulfilment of the God-given personality. His grace is given through recognizable signs: the visible marks of the visible Church.

6

HOLY BAPTISM

Membership and Commitment
Sign and Gift
Man's Response
Infant Baptism
Confirmation
Other Churches

Membership and Commitment

THE font is normally found near the door of the church. Its position symbolizes the fact that Baptism is the gateway through which we enter into the Family of God. Through Baptism we become part of the great fellowship of all faithful people living under the special influence of the Holy Spirit. Corporate membership of the Body of Christ begins at the font.

Immediately after the Baptism proper, the priest marks the child with the sign of the Cross using these wonderfully expressive words:

> *We receive this child into the congregation of Christ's flock and do sign him with the sign of the Cross, in token that hereafter he shall not be ashamed to confess the faith of Christ crucified, and manfully to fight under his banner, against sin, the world and the devil; and to continue Christ's faithful soldier and servant unto his life's end.*

The Cross marks him as Christ's man. The words express the fact that he is bound in a personal relationship with Christ involving total commitment for life. So it is as a child of God that he enters the Family. And it is as a member of the Family that he is made Christ's.

Here then are the complementary characteristics of all baptized Christians – *personal commitment* and *corporate membership*. They reflect Christ's summary of the Law which demands the response of man's love, personally to God and corporately to all other men.

Sign and Gift

The outward and visible sign of Baptism is the water which is normally poured over the candidate's head. The action is invariably accompanied by the invocation of the Trinity:
.... in the Name of the Father, and of the Son, and of the Holy Ghost.

In Jewish and Christian tradition the ceremonial use of water has often been associated with the washing away of sins. It is in this respect that the sign suggests the gift of Baptism. During the service, prayer is made that the water may be sanctified *to the mystical washing away of sin.* Under the Holy Spirit the water becomes an effectual sign conveying to the candidate the gift of death to sin and resurrection to new life in Christ.

Thus in her admission of new members the Church regularly relives and makes available to men the fruits of Christ's redeeming death and resurrection. St Paul reminds us that :

> *.... when we were baptized into union with Christ Jesus we were baptized into his death. By Baptism we were buried with him, and lay dead, in order that, as Christ was raised from the dead in the splendour of the Father, so also we might set our feet upon the new path of life.*

Above all *raised*, for it is the *rising* which is the immeasurable gift. Immeasurable, because it is no less than the life of the risen Lord implanted in the new member. Henceforth he may live in the power of the Spirit. He has *the power of God and the wisdom of God* which alone can correct his inclination to sin.

Man's Response

There is no magic about this or any other sacramental gift. God gives: man may accept or reject. Man's choice makes no difference to the reality of the gift. The extent to which the gift becomes effective in his life does, however, depend upon his response. According to the Book of Common Prayer man's response includes repentance, trust and obedience.

Repentance is his sincere desire and intention to turn from sin to God and the good life which he wills for all men;

Trust is his acknowledgment of his dependence on God who made him: a son's reliance on the Father who knows his deepest needs;

Obedience is man's offering of his will to God to persevere in living his life in sacrificial devotion to God's purpose: after the pattern of our Lord he says: *Not my will, but thine, be done.*

Response involves personal commitment. Commitment involves the decision to share in Christ's death to sin. Death to sin is the gateway to newness of life. So may the gift become effective in man's life. So may he, like Christ and with Christ, rise again to true fellowship with God and man.

Infant Baptism

Though increasing numbers of adults seek Baptism today, the normal practice is for children to be baptized in infancy. Why is this so when infants patently cannot make the sort of response just discussed?

Historically, infant baptism has been a feature of Church life from earliest times. According to the New Testament whole households were baptized, and these would normally include children as well as slaves.

Socially and personally, few Christian families would wish to deny their children the spiritual benefits they themselves enjoy. Rather they would wish their children to come as soon as possible into the full fellowship of the Church.

Practically, therefore, the Church places the responsibility for response fairly and squarely upon *parents*, *godparents*, and *the whole adult congregation*. Upon them rests the burden of ensuring that the child is so nurtured and encouraged by precept and example as to grow continually in the knowledge and love of God. Then he may, on reaching years of discretion, make his own response with conviction and sincerity.

Confirmation

Confirmation is the occasion when the candidate publicly professes his own response of repentance, trust and obedience, which earlier had been promised by others on his behalf at Baptism.

The sacrament is administered by the bishop through the laying on of hands with prayer. The candidate receives the strengthening gift of the Holy Spirit to live the rest of his life according to God's will and he is admitted to Holy Communion.

He may now be said to have attained adult status in the Church, carrying full responsibility, freely sought and accepted, as an active member of the Body of Christ. So the bishop prays to God that he *may continue thine for ever and daily increase in thy Holy Spirit more and more.*

Although Baptism is generally regarded as finding its completion in Confirmation, the administration of both raises problems as to their proper interpretation and practice. The whole pattern and process of Christian initiation is at present under consideration.

Other Churches

Baptism with water in the Name of the Trinity is acknowledged and practised by all the main Christian bodies, except the Society of Friends and the Salvation Army which do not observe the Sacraments. The Baptist Church, however, does not accept *infant* Baptism. They hold instead that the only true and original form of the Sacrament is *believers'* Baptism, that is, of those who have reached an age when they can personally confess their faith and undertake the appropriate vows for themselves.

The Orthodox Churches administer *Chrism*, that is, anointing with holy oils blessed by the bishops. This is preceded by the Baptism of the infant and followed by his admission to Holy Communion.

The Roman Church practises infant Baptism as the norm. At about the age of seven the child is admitted to Holy Communion, for which Confirmation is not necessary. This follows two or three years later at the hands of the bishop.

Some Lutheran Churches administer Confirmation through the Office of the local pastor, though it is still the gateway to Communion. A similar practice exists in the Presbyterian Church of Scotland. Other Lutheran Churches, for example the Swedish Church with which we are in communion, have bishops who administer Confirmation.

The Methodist Church normally admits to Communion after instruction and admission to membership status.

Thus all Christian bodies which practise infant Baptism have some second rite which is regarded as completing Baptism and which has at the heart of it personal confession of faith and, with the exception of the Roman Church, admission to Communion. Although customarily administered within the local congregation, admission to membership is generally interpreted as admission to membership of the whole Church of Christ.

Differences arise over three points:

(i) *as to what precisely happens after Baptism;*

(ii) *as to who administers the second rite;*

(iii) *as to when admission to Communion takes place, and why.*

These raise the fundamental question of what we understand by Christian Initiation. How precisely are men brought into the full membership and communicant life of the Church? What exactly was the teaching and practice of the primitive Church regarding it? It is along the lines of discussing the pattern and process of initiation as a whole that much fruitful reconsideration of differences about Baptism is now developing.

7

HOLY COMMUNION

In His Presence

THIS is where we begin, for we believe that under the effectual signs of bread and wine our Lord is truly present. The Sacrament of Holy Communion proclaims and embodies his Presence.

Of course we do not fully understand nor can we precisely define it. Our sufficient authority is Jesus himself who said: *This is my Body . . . . this is my Blood.* The Anglican refuses to go further and attempt a closer description. There is an intellectual honesty about this refusal which is illustrated in a verse attributed to Queen Elizabeth I:

> *His was the Word that spake it,*
> *He took the Bread and brake it,*
> *And what his Word doth make it,*
> *That I believe and take it.*

Attempts to popularize and extend the Parish Communion with a sense of community, by the encouragement of numbers, or by the stimulus of modern music, may fail, unless all are directed upwards to him under whose shadow we worship and in whose Presence we can but say:

> *Look, Father, look on his anointed face,*
> *And only look on us as found in him.*

In the Sacrament Christ himself acts in his Body gathered together. In so far as he acts and we gather together in his Presence we may be said to be truly worshipping. So the Eucharist is the action of Christ continuing in his Church.

This is the central fact which overshadows what we may

make of the Eucharist. It matters more what the Eucharist makes of us as we humbly enter his Presence and accept the gift that is offered.

The Gift

As the Lord commanded, we take and break and bless bread; we pour and bless wine. We have given and acted. We receive back far more than we have given.

Under the Holy Spirit the bread becomes the gift of his Body; wine becomes his Blood. Not in any material sense but in the sense that now both elements are charged with spiritual significance for the faithful worshipper.

Again Christ is the centre, not ourselves. He is the Host. We are the guests at his Table. Here he gives himself, crucified, risen, glorified, that we may in truth and in deed feed on him. The words spoken by the priest as he administers to the communicant are eloquent:

The Body of our Lord Jesus Christ which was given for thee . . . . feed on Him.

Countless thousands of Christians have found this to be true in their own experience. Their experience would lead them to speak with gratitude of this gift as offering, among others, three things:

Forgiveness: Christ died for us that we might be forgiven. In receiving his Life in Holy Communion, we receive both the condemnation and the forgiveness of sins. Here we know both the hatred of sin which is of God's nature and his out-reaching love which forgives the erring son 'while he is yet a great way off'. Here is both pain and bliss. Here as nowhere else the communicant faces the Cross of Christ. Here his conscience is both smitten and strengthened, chastened and purified, above all because he is offered forgiveness and can sing with sincerity:

> *In the Cross of Christ I glory*
> *Towering o'er the wrecks of time . . . .*
>
> *Bane and blessing, pain and pleasure*
> *By the Cross are sanctified;*
> *Peace is there that knows no measure,*
> *Joys that through all time abide.*

Strength: The Comfortable Words of the Prayer Book Service are *strengthening* words. And it is this encounter with Christ in the Sacrament which strengthens men to live their lives aright and find the happiness God intends. In feeding on him we share in his life. Because in his earthly life he was *tempted in all things like as we are,* he knows our temptations and weaknesses. Because he was *yet without sin,* he also knows the way to victory over both. So as we feed on him we are indeed strengthened in weakness, supported in temptation, and upheld in endeavour. In him we pray:

> *Father, hear the prayer we offer.*
> *Not for ease that prayer shall be,*
> *But for strength that we may ever*
> *Live our lives courageously.*

Fellowship: Fellowship above all with Christ and his Church militant here on earth and triumphant in heaven. Not alone does the communicant come to the altar. He comes in his Master's presence, with angels and archangels and all the company of heaven as well as his fellow communicants. Note the order. All else flows from Christ's own Presence. It is because of this that we are at once lifted into the timeless worship of heaven and belong to an earthly community in which race and rank matter not, and only love and service count. Caught up in this sacramental action we bear witness that:

> *One Family, we dwell in Him:*
> *One Church, above, beneath.*

Man's Acceptance

The Invitation which follows the Prayer for the Church in the Communion Service speaks of the manner of man's acceptance of the gift of Christ's sacramental Presence:

Repentance: Time and again man must undertake this salutary exercise; for time and again he falls short of his glorious calling as a son of God. Above all he must practise it as he comes to Communion. It is not enough to have frequent communion and large numbers attending. The corporate act of the congregation involves each individual member of it in a personal encounter with God which calls for preparation, prayer and penitence. Each must come with the humble cry of the publican: *God be merciful to me, a sinner.*

Love: The communicant must also come in love and charity with all men. St John reminds us that we can hardly claim to love God whom we cannot see, if all the time we hate our brother whom we do see. We come to the Sacrament of unity which unites God and man, and man with man. So man must strive to come with love in his heart and charity in his actions: forgiving others as he himself expects God to forgive him. Above all, he will come with sorrow for the divisions which separate Christians at the very point where they should be one, and seen to be one.

Faith: The Invitation exhorts us to 'draw near *with faith*'. So it must be. We are to have the self-abandonment of an Augustine who knew so well that his soul was restless until it found its rest in God. We must come with the simple faith of the child who was anxious that God should take care of himself, *because*, he added, *without you we should be sunk*. Independence must be exchanged for the dependence which casts all its care on him, for he indeed careth for us. We approach with lively faith in God's mercies, nothing doubting.

The Centrality of Christ

How then does the Church perform this great act of worship? She does so by *looking unto Jesus, the author and finisher of our faith*. Christ is the centre and heart of all that happens in the Eucharist. So we celebrate the Sacrament by obeying Christ, by remembering Christ, by thanking Christ, by participating in Christ's Sacrifice:

by obeying Christ's own command to *Do this* in remembrance of him. The same thought is emphasized in the Prayer of Oblation when what has been done is described as *our bounden duty*. In this act above all priest and people are exercising that godly obedience which they undertook at Baptism;

by remembering Christ's great deliverance of man from the power of sin through his Cross and Passion. The Jews were careful to remember their own great deliverance from Egypt by keeping the Passover Feast. They remembered that it was God who delivered them, made them into a people and sealed them in a covenant relationship with him. Christians remember the new covenant made in Christ's blood by which they are sealed in a binding relationship to him and each other as the New Israel of God. The new covenant was instituted at the Last Supper, and so each celebration of the Lord's Supper is a recalling of the historical facts of Christ's redeeming act and the benefits we derive therefrom. Like St Paul we *proclaim the Lord's death till he come;*

by thanking Christ for his infinite love. We cannot recall the Good News of his Cross and Resurrection without involuntarily bursting into the *praise and thanksgiving* of the Prayer of Oblation. The sheer wonder of it is still almost too much for human imagination:

> *It is a thing most wonderful,*
> *Almost too wonderful to be,*
> *That God's own Son should come from heaven,*
> *And die to save a child like me.*

The whole Service is one of thanksgiving and so it is often called the Eucharist. It ends appropriately with the great hymn of praise: *Glory be to God on High* . . . .

by participating in Christ's Sacrifice. We do so conscious of the priority of what Christ himself has done, once for all. We do so under the shadow of his Cross. Christ himself, the great High Priest, is the true Celebrant uniting his Church with him in the eternal pleading of his once-for-all Sacrifice.   In him and through him we plead the Eucharistic Sacrifice. *We offer it,* says the last Lambeth Report, *only because he has offered the one Sacrifice, once for all, in which we need to participate.* Only so may we dare to identify ourselves with him and offer *ourselves, our souls and bodies* to the Father to undertake a life of Christlike sacrifice and service.

Other Churches

At this point differences between the Churches widen. The Church of Rome goes further in defining the mystery of the Sacrament in terms of the doctrine of transubstantiation. Roman eucharistic practice is also still affected by a doctrine of sacrifice which permits the offering of Mass by the individual priest rather than the assembled Church.

Among Reformed Churches there is considerable variation as to the relationship of the Real Presence to the elements of bread and wine. The Lutheran Small Catechism seems to indicate a position near to our own, while some English Free Churches would place emphasis upon the whole enactment of the Communion Service.

It is true that the revival of sacramental worship in recent years has cut across not only party lines within Churches but also across denominational barriers. This is heartening and it is matched by an increase in liturgical scholarship and the doctrinal study of the Eucharist.

The problem of growing together, however, remains. We are deeply divided over the place of the Holy Communion in any approach to unity. There are two opposing views. The one, widely held in the Anglican Church, is that it is the Sacrament of Unity and, as such, is the goal of our efforts to come together. Thus we cannot in honesty participate in Holy Communion with members of other Churches not in communion with ourselves until we reach a wide measure of agreement on the essentials of the Faith. The other view, found in many Reformed Churches, is that Holy Communion is the legitimate means to unity. Here, they say, all who love the Lord Jesus in sincerity may participate and in doing so learn more quickly to grow together.

We cannot fully appreciate these and other differences without reference to the doctrine of the ordained Ministry to which we turn next.

8

THE ORDAINED MINISTRY

The Threefold Ministry

WE possess a threefold Ministry of Bishops, Priests and Deacons. They are selected, set apart and given authority through Ordination. The form of the Ordering of Bishops, Priests and Deacons occurs towards the end of our Prayer Book. It is a carefully preserved document in which it is clear that men are ordained through the laying on of hands by bishops with prayer, so that they receive the grace of the Holy Spirit and the authority of the whole Church to perform their several functions. As these functions are not always clearly understood, it is worth listing them:

A *Bishop* is the Chief Pastor with special responsibility for guarding the Church's teaching. His peculiar functions include those of consecrating other bishops, ordaining priests and making deacons; and of confirming.

A *Priest* is a Minister of the Word and Sacraments. His peculiar functions include the celebration of Holy Communion and the pronouncement of absolution. He has the spiritual charge, called cure of souls, of all those committed to him.

A *Deacon* assists the priest, particularly in the administration of the Sacrament, in preaching and visiting the sick.

The Bishops

Bishops, collectively referred to as the *episcopate*, are the key-stone. Our Church is an episcopal Church, not simply because episcopacy is a convenient form of government, but rather because it is regarded as *the principle of unity in teaching and sacraments*. So it appears to have been in the very early days of the undivided Church. Anglican belief is that consecration of bishops and ordination by bishops have their roots in Apostolic practice and custom. Archbishop Garbett has put it succinctly:

> *Only those who have been duly consecrated by other bishops have the right to ordain to the priesthood and the diaconate, and only those who have been so ordained have the right to preach authoritatively the Word of God and to administer the Sacraments in the Church of England.*
>
> *It is for this reason that the utmost care was taken in Queen Elizabeth's reign to see that the new Archbishop was consecrated by those who themselves had been duly consecrated.*
>
> *It is one of the distinguishing marks of the Anglican Church that, with the exception of the Church of Sweden, it is the only reformed Church which has preserved the historic episcopate.*

The fourth point in the Lambeth Quadrilateral makes it clear that it is not only the inward call of the Spirit claimed by the individual that is required of an ordained minister, but also the sanction of Christ and of the Church at large. The actual words are:

> *A Ministry acknowledged by every part of the Church as possessing not only the inward call of the Spirit, but also the commission of Christ and the authority of the whole Body.*

Traditional Anglican belief sees the commission of Christ and the authority of the Church focussed upon and transmitted through the Order of Bishops. There is a great weight of evidence in the writings of the Fathers of the undivided Church to support this. Among them the Bishops were indeed the key-stone. They were the guardians of true doctrine: the heirs of the Apostles in whose teaching the Church of the New Testament *continued steadfastly*.

This is the traditional and still the majority view within the Church of England. It is only just, however, to add that differing emphases are placed on episcopacy by various sections of the Church. While always seeking to be loyal to Scripture and Tradition, our Church tries at the same time to allow a proper freedom in discussion and the expression of opinion. By this refusal to stifle reason the Church may remain alive to new directions and emphases which may, under the Holy Spirit, become apparent in her continuing work in a rapidly changing world.

Structure and Government

No society, but above all the society which claims to be the Body of Christ, can operate effectively without a seemly ordering of its affairs. What has just been discussed is concerned with the vital question of *Church Order*, that is, the whole *structure and government of the Church*. Throughout the greater part of the history of the Christian Church, it has been upon structure and government that her unity in teaching and sacrament has depended. This is why the resolving of problems concerning the Ministry intimately affect areas of doctrine such as those of Christian Initiation and Holy Communion.

Consideration of structure and government drives us to delve deeper still into just what we mean and understand by 'The Church'. This is the root question. There is no room in the short compass of this publication to deal with all that this involves. For our immediate purpose we have concentrated on the ordained Ministry. When, however, we speak of 'The Church', this quite definitely includes a *ministry of lay people* who, with the clergy, share in the work of extending the Kingdom of God. As Archbishop Fisher has put it:

> .... *and the laity are one with them (i.e., the clergy) in the work of the Church in which all are a royal priesthood, a consecrated nation* ....

We thus subscribe to the *priesthood of all believers*. This belief has been emphasized in recent years by many attempts to involve the laity in more active roles in the work of the Church. In the journey towards the reunion of all Christian people the application of this conviction to Church structure and government will be important. The Church of England has already been reminded by her Presbyterian neighbours of the necessity of giving practical expression to her professed acceptance of this teaching of St Peter.

Other Churches

Our possession of the threefold Ministry links us with the ancient Western Church. We share this possession with the Orthodox Churches. The Church of Rome also possesses a Ministry of Bishops, Priests and Deacons, though she refuses to recognize a similar possession on our part. However, she superimposes on her own threefold structure the office of the Papacy. This means that the Pope, when speaking as Head of the Church, is believed to be infallible.

Some Lutheran Churches possess bishops, but only the Swedish Church has retained the historic episcopate. Other Lutheran Churches, the Presbyterian Church and the English Free Churches have a single Ministry. All stress the inward call of the Spirit and the commission of the Church. In Baptist and Congregational Churches the commission is normally conveyed in the setting of the local congregation. In the Methodist Church it is conveyed by the President in Conference; in Presbyterian Churches by the Presbytery.

Our relations with the Western Churches in this respect are more than anything else a matter of recognition. In the cases of the Presbyterian Church and the English Free Churches, the differences are greater. The actual words of the Lambeth Quadrilateral present little difficulty. Their interpretation within the Anglican Church to mean a ministry ordained by bishops standing in the historic succession is the hurdle which the Free Churches have found most difficult to surmount.

Thank God the days of mutual recrimination have passed. At their height they were most sinful in relation to opposing views about the Ministry. A new landmark was reached in 1920 when the Lambeth Conference of that year pronounced that the non-episcopal ministries *have been manifestly blessed and owned by the Holy Spirit as effective means of grace*. The Anglican concern has been and is, not with the condemning of other ministries, but with maintaining such elements of the undivided Church as their continuity in history seems to indicate correspond most nearly to the purpose of God. Of these the episcopate seems to be one, more particularly in regard to visible unity.

APPENDICES

The Anglican Communion
Catholic and Reformed
Comprehensive
Establishment
The 39 Articles

I. The Anglican Communion

WE have been speaking of the Church of England. But we cannot set this in its correct perspective without reference to the Anglican Communion to which the Church of England gave birth.

The great missionary societies of the Church bear witness to her zeal to spread the Gospel to all nations. As a result of the past and present labours of these societies there are, in most countries of the world, Anglican Churches usually arranged in bishoprics or provinces. Whatever may have been true in the past, they now form a formidable group of self-governing Churches which are voluntarily in communion with the See of Canterbury. Together they form the Anglican Communion.

Like the Churches of the first few centuries after Christ, they have no visible or formal head, nor are they held together by an administrative system. Together they share the essentials of the Catholic and Reformed Faith of the Church of England. Their chief personal link is the Archbishop of Canterbury who invites them at ten-year intervals to the Lambeth Conference for mutual consultation. We may stress the word *consultation*, for the findings and recommendations of the Conference, consisting of all bishops of the Anglican Communion, while they have considerable influence on Anglican thought throughout the world, are not binding on any member Church.

The nature of the Anglican Communion was defined by the Lambeth Conference of 1930 as follows:

The Anglican Communion is a fellowship, within the One, Holy, Catholic and Apostolic Church, of those duly constituted Dioceses, Provinces or Regional Churches in communion with the See of Canterbury, which have the following characteristics in common:

(a) They uphold and propagate the Catholic and Apostolic Faith and Order as they are generally set forth in the Book of Common Prayer as authorized in their several Churches;

(b) They are particular or national Churches, and as such promote within each of their territories a national expression of christian faith, life and worship;

(c) They are bound together not by a central legislative and executive authority, but by mutual loyalty sustained through the common counsel of the Bishops in Conference.

II. Catholic and Reformed

The Church of England is both, and never one without the other:

She is *Catholic* in the sense defined in Chapter I, possessing the Catholic Scriptures, Creeds, Sacraments and Ministry. All these the Church has studiously retained at and since the Reformation.

She is *Reformed* in four major respects:

She is free from the domination of the Pope whose infallible authority she repudiates;

She gives freedom to the individual in matters of worship and intellect; there is a minimum of the word *must*, *may* occuring much more frequently;

She affords free access to the Scriptures in English;

She maintains simplicity of congregational worship.

Both elements are contained within the Church and are held in balance or in tension. The true Anglican position cannot otherwise be stated or accepted.

Because of this, we preserve links with a wide variety of Churches. For example, as *Catholic* we have obvious links with the Orthodox and Roman Churches, and as *Reformed* or *Protestant* we have definite links with the Lutheran Churches as well as the Presbyterian Church and the Free Churches in this country. This gives us a special responsibility in the search for reunion, and we have often been called the 'Bridge Church'.

III. Comprehensive

Ever since the Elizabethan Settlement in the 16th century, ours has been a Church containing within its fold a wide variety of shades of churchmanship. Indeed, a Church which is both *Catholic* and *Reformed*, and gives considerable spiritual and intellectual freedom to the individual, cannot but be comprehensive. So we find to-day Anglicans who term themselves high, low, middle, broad or simply churchmen with no particular or party allegiance.

Whilst there was once bitterness between different levels of churchmanship, there is now a growing understanding and fellowship among them. This is evidence of the unity in diversity which is of the true nature of Anglicanism. Indeed, each diverse element has its own contribution to make to the whole, as Archbishop Garbett wrote as long ago as 1947:

The Anglo-Catholics have given it rich ideals of worship and of churchmanship, and restored to it a deeper sense of the meaning of the sacramental life: the Evangelicals have kept alive in it a burning love for the conversion of souls and for the winning of the world for Christ: the Liberals have witnessed to the necessity of bringing all modern thought into the Service of the Master, and of using the intellect in the presentation of Christian truth. Our Church would be infinitely the poorer if any one of these parties were ostracized or expelled.

Such diversity, if it is to be comprehended in an overall unity, demands the cheerful acceptance of tensions embraced with a tenderness born of charity, for this is the spirit of Anglicanism.

IV. Establishment

The Church of England is the established Church of this land, that is, she has close links with, and legal attachments to, the State. The connection goes back a long way in history and was intensified at the Reformation.

It is seen at its most edifying in the Coronation Service when the principal figures are the Queen and the Archbishop of Canterbury. The Queen is present in the dual capacity of Head of State and Defender of the Faith. In the Service the dependence of the Queen, and of the State of which she is head, upon God himself is clearly proclaimed in words and ceremonial.

It is seen at its most embarrassing in the fact that the Church must submit her promulgation of doctrine and worship to Parliament for approval. Further, the Queen through the Prime Minister, acting in consultation with the Archbishop of Canterbury, appoints bishops. Parliamentary control of doctrine and worship is exercised wisely and with restraint; the system of making episcopal appointments has also much to commend it in practice. Some, however, would object to any form of State control over the affairs of the Church on the grounds of principle, as well as on the practical grounds of the danger of a Government hostile to the Church.

Many, however, who wish for disestablishment also hold that to work for it now would involve the Church in such a long process of legal enactments that her energies would be expended unwisely at a time when they should be used for the urgent business of proclaiming the Gospel in the world.

One thing establishment does not do, and that is to provide money for the coffers of the Church! The Church as a society does not receive a penny from the State. Only individuals in the direct employ of the Government, such as Prison and Service Chaplains, are paid by the State.

V. The 39 Articles

The 39 Articles of religion are printed with the Book of Common Prayer. They arose out of the controversies of the 16th century and set out the position adopted by the Church of England as against Rome and the extreme Protestants at that time. Thought has changed so much that the Articles contain a good deal which it is difficult to accept in the same terms to-day, and a good deal which is outdated. It must, however, be remembered that the Articles are not binding upon the laity, and since 1865 the clergy do not sign the Articles but give a general assent to the doctrine contained in them and in the Prayer Book.

The Articles give the historical position of the Church of England in a 16th century setting. It is, on the other hand, the Creeds which give the faith of the Church to which all her members are bound.

CLASSIFIED READING LIST

Devotional
The Church of England
Other Churches
The Bible
Tradition
Reason
The Creeds
The Prayer Book
The Sacraments
The Ordained Ministry

1. DEVOTIONAL

Of the Imitation of Christ	Thomas à Kempis	Nelson
A Serious Call to a Devout and Holy Life	William Law	Epworth
The Practice of the Presence of God	Brother Lawrence	Epworth
The Crown of the Year	Austin Farrer	Black
Lord I Believe	Austin Farrer	Faith Press
The Lord's Prayer	W. R. Matthews	Hodder and Stoughton
My God, My Glory	E. Milner-White	S.P.C.K.
A Procession of Passion Prayers	E. Milner-White	S.P.C.K.
The Life of Prayer	Von Hugel	Dent

2. THE CHURCH OF ENGLAND

Anglicanism	J. W. C. Wand	Weiderfeld and Nicolson
What the Church of England Stands For	J. W. C. Wand	Mowbray
The Christian Religion Explained	Bishop Wand and Others	Mowbray
The Church of England	Hensley Henson	C.U.P.
The Faith, History and Practice of the Church of England	A. W. Eaton	Hodder and Stoughton
Everyman's Book about the English Church	F. C. Happold	Faber
A History of the Church in England	J. R. H. Moorman	Black
Unity, Uniformity and the English Church	S. C. Clark	Mowbray
The Claims of the Church of England	C. F. Garbett	Hodder and Stoughton
The Church of England To-day	C. F. Garbett	Hodder and Stoughton
The Call of God	H. G. G. Herklots	Hodder and Stoughton

The English Religious Tradition	Norman Sykes	S.C.M.
The Doctrine of the Church of England	Archbishops' Commission	S.P.C.K.
The Church and People	C. S. Carpenter	S.P.C.K.
The Churchman's Heritage	E. G. Knapp-Fisher	Black
The Meaning of Churchmanship	K. D. Mackenzie	Mowbray
The Duties of a Churchman	R. C. Mortimer	Black
The Life and Writings of Jeremy Taylor	C. J. Stranks	S.P.C.K.
William Temple	F. A. Iremonger	O.U.P.
Headlam	Ronald Jaspar	Faith Press
Cyril Foster Garbett	Charles Smythe	Hodder and Stoughton
What's the Use?	S. J. Forrester	Mowbray
Poems in the Porch	John Betjeman	S.P.C.K.

3. OTHER CHURCHES

Barriers to Unity	M. Bruce	Faith Press
Documents on Christian Unity	G. K. A. Bell	O.U.P.
The Churches and the Church	B. Leening	Darton, Longman Todd
The Ecumenical Movement	Kenneth Slack	Edinburgh House Press
The Ecumenical Movement	Goodall	O.U.P.
20th Century Christianity	Stephen Neill	Collins
The British Churches Today	Kenneth Slack	S.C.M.
Catholicity	E. S. Abbott	Black
The Protestant Tradition	J. S. Whale	C.U.P.

The Divine Liturgy of the Russian Orthodox Church	N. W. Gogol	Darton, Longman Todd
Roman Catholicism in England	E. W. Watkin	O.U.P.
The Council and Reunion	Hans Kung	Sheed and Ward
The Riddle of Roman Catholicism	Jaroslav Pelikan	Hodder and Stoughton
Presbyterianism	John M. Barclay	Belfast
The English Free Churches	Horton Davies	O.U.P.
This is Methodism	F. H. Everson	Epworth
Congregationalism	D. Jenkins	Faber
What Baptists stand for	H. Cook	Carey Kingsgate Press
The Beginnings of Quakerism	W. C. Braithwaite	C.U.P.

4. THE BIBLE

Is the Bible Inspired ?	J. Burnaby	S.P.C.K.
The Authority of the Bible	C. H. Dodd	Fontana
On the Authority of the Bible	D. E. Ninehan	S.P.C.K.
The Story of the Bible	F. G. Kenyon	Murray
The Plain Man Looks at the Bible	William Neil	Fontana
The Rediscovery of the Bible	William Neil	Hodder and Stoughton
Teach Yourself Guide Book to the Bible	Alice Parmelee	E.U.P.
The Bible Word Book	R. Tatlock	Mowbray
Scripture and Faith	A. G. Hebert	Bles
The Bible in an Age of Science	A. Richardson	S.C.M.
The Old Testament as the Word of God	S. Mowinckel	Blackwell
The Authority of the Old Testament	A. G. Hebert	Faber

The Throne of David	A. G. Hebert	Faber
A Layman's Guide to the Old Testament	P. S. Robinson	S.P.C.K.
Readings in St John's Gospel	William Temple	Macmillan
According to the Scriptures	C. H. Dodd	Nisbet
The Apostolic Preaching and its Development	C. H. Dodd	Hodder and Stoughton
The Meaning of Paul for To-day	C. H. Dodd	Fontana
The Kingdom of God in the experience of Jesus	S. H. Hooke	Duckworth
The Riddle of the New Testament	Hoskins and Davey	Faber
St John's Gospel	R. H. Lightfoot	O.U.P.
A Man called Jesus	J. B. Phillips	Bles
Jesus, Master and Lord	H. E. W. Turner	Mowbray
A New Way of Looking at the Gospels	D. E. Ninehan	S.P.C.K.

5. TRADITION

The Interpretation of the Bible	J. D. Wood	Duckworth
The Early Christian Fathers	H. Bettenson	O.U.P.
The Early Christian Fathers	F. L. Cross	Duckworth
Fathers and Heretics	G. L. Prestige	S.P.C.K.
A New Eusebius	J. Stevenson	S.P.C.K.
The Documents of the Christian Church	H. Bettenson	O.U.P.
The Life in the Early Church	A. E. Wellsford	S.P.C.K.

6. REASON

Science and Christian Belief	C. A. Coulson	Fontana

Science and the Idea of God	C. A. Coulson	C.U.P.
Science, Technology and the Christian	C. A. Coulson	Epworth
Faith for Modern Man	A. N. Gilkes	Faber
The Faith of a Physicist	H. E. Huntley	Bles
The Sense of History: Secular and Sacred	M. C. D'Arcy	Faber
Christianity and History	H. Butterfield	Fontana
Towards a Christian Philosophy	L. Hodgson	Nisbet
The Purpose of God	W. R. Matthews	Nisbet
Nature, Man and God	William Temple	Macmillan
Beyond Personality	C. S. Lewis	Bles
Broadcast Talks	C. S. Lewis	Bles
Mere Christianity	C. S. Lewis	Fontana
Miracles	C. S. Lewis	Fontana
Transposition and Other Addresses	C. S. Lewis	Bles

7. THE CREEDS

Thinking through the Creed	H. Burnaby	Hodder and Stoughton
Creeds in the Making	A. R. Richardson	S.C.M.
History of the Creeds	F. J. Badcock	S.P.C.K.
The Apostles' Creed	A. E. Burn	Ribbington
Articles of Thy Belief	Caroline Adams	S.P.C.K.
Christian Belief	R. H. Malden	S.P.C.K.
The Faith Today	M. Stockwood	S.P.C.K.
Belief of Christendom	J. Burnaby	S.P.C.K.
Christian Doctrine	J. S. Whale	Fontana
God was in Christ	D. Baillie	Faber
The Resurrection of Christ	A. M. Ramsey	Fontana

8. THE PRAYER BOOK

The Book of Common Prayer	D. E. W. Harrison	S.P.C.K.
The Story of the Prayer Book	Johnstone and Evans	Mowbray

The Story of the Prayer Book	P. Dearmer	O.U.P.
Christian Use of the Psalms	H. De Candole	Mowbray
Liturgy and Worship	W. K. Lowther-Clarke	S.P.C.K.
Liturgy and Society	A. G. Hebert	Faber
Liturgy coming to Life	J. A. T. Robinson	Mowbray

9. THE SACRAMENTS

The Spirit, the Church and the Sacraments	J. G. Davies	Faith Press
The Theology of the Sacraments	D. Baillie	Faber
Baptism and Confirmation	Liturgical Commission Report	S.P.C.K.
One Lord One Baptism	Faith and Order Reports	S.C.M.
The New Testament Doctrine of Baptism	W. F. Flemington	S.P.C.K.
Receive this Child	E. W. Southcott	Mowbray
Theology of Confirmation in relation to Baptism	Gregory Dix	Black
Confirmation	L. S. Thornton	Black
Holy Communion and Holy Spirit	J. E. L. Oulton	S.P.C.K.
The Sacrifice of Christ	C. F. D. Moule	Hodder and Stoughton
Covenant and Sacrifice	Basil Minchin	Longmans
At the Lord's Table	Cosslett Quin	Lutterworth

10. THE ORDAINED MINISTRY

Why Bishops ?	H. E. W. Turner	C.I.O.
The Historic Episcopate	Kenneth Carey	Black

The Question of Anglican Orders	Gregory Dix	Black
Old Priest and New Presbyter	Norman Sykes	C.U.P.
Vocation and Ministry	F. R. Barry	Nisbet
Asking the Right Questions	F. R. Barry	Hodder and Stoughton
Ministry and Priesthood	T. W. Manson	Epworth
The Household of God	Lesslie Newbigin	S.C.M.
A Theology of the Laity	Hendrik Kraemer	Lutterworth

PRINTED
BY

36 STEWARD ST
LONDON E.1

PUBLISHED BY THE CHURCH INFORMATION OFFICE FOR THE
CHURCH OF ENGLAND YOUTH COUNCIL
69 GT PETER STREET, WESTMINSTER, SW1
© The Central Board of Finance of the Church of England, 1962